DISCARD

Chaco Trilogy

CHACO
Trilogy

V.B. Price

La Alameda Press • Albuquerque

Cover photograph: "Fajada Butte"—Kirk Gittings
Text photographs: "Petroglyphs, Chaco"—J.B. Bryan

ISBN: 1-888809-10-8
Library of Congress Number: 98-067349

First Edition

La Alameda Press
9636 Guadalupe Trail NW
Albuquerque, New Mexico 87114

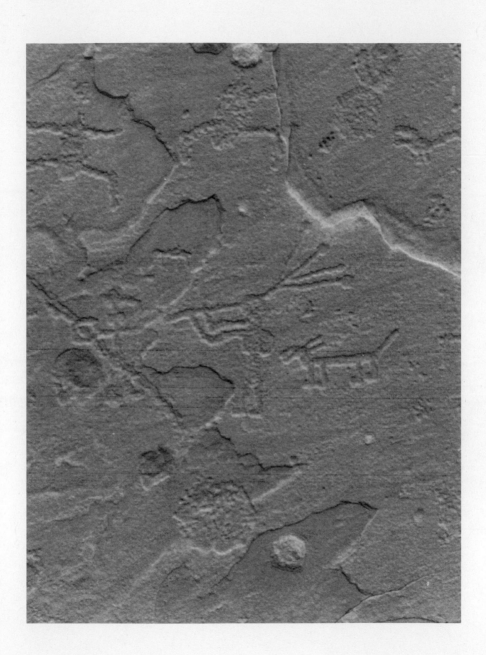

CONTENTS

I've never been drawn so irresistibly and consistently to any place—or almost to any person—as I have to Chaco Canyon over the last 20 years. Its attraction has never weakened, my feelings have never cooled. The source of Chaco's magnetic and transformative energies remains mysterious to me. And even my poems about it seem to me at times like sand piling up around an invisible object. But Chaco's power is as undeniable to me as apparently it was to ancestral Pueblo peoples. Its spiritual gravity concentrates attention and emotion so forcefully that they undergo a metamorphosis, emerging combined as an imaginative fluidity, a mercurial richness that can adapt to anything.

When I'm in Chaco Canyon I'm there so completely that what happens to *it* happens to *me*. And even though my stamina and optimism are always tested, nothing goes wrong in Chaco; it is its own totality; it admits of nothing being out of place; what is there and what will be there is as perfect as what has been there. Even if I were to die there, it would not be an accident, a rupture in the pattern of my life; nothing would be wrong. So to be in Chaco Canyon can be wearingly hard but safe, arduous but effortless, dependable but unpredictable; it is both mortal and infinite; peaceful, chaotic, and perpetual; loved, longed for, and fulfilling.

I slip down the north road into the canyon with the same ease as I slip into a booth at lunch across from windfall friends, those whose presences alone create an atmosphere that reveals to me the possibility of my entirety. Like their voices and the maps of their minds, the canyon's life creates in me both desire and contentment. It's impossible to resist it—the character of its light and the disposition of its shadows, its cloud tones, haziness, heat, the quality of its seclusion, its suddenness and vulnerability. I feel like Sappho with the canyon and with the friends of my life. My interest is immediate, luxurious, releasing; I can't put my attention anywhere else; I can't help but feel myself unlock, revivify. I am as satisfied with them as Sappho was with "cool feet and slenderest knees."

Some places and people are our optimum habitats, our ideal conditions. We thrive with them, reviving over and over. We always return. With them, thresholds are never crossed; boundaries expand just as we try to move beyond them, carrying us with them further and further into the fullness of ourselves and one another. With metamorphosis we can never become what we're not. Only force perverts fulfillment. Parasitic force: it has nothing to do with love or Chaco Canyon.

When I first visited Chaco in 1960, it made little impression. I was studying anthropology as an undergraduate, preoccupied with the conundrums of my own culture, but still oddly curious about Pueblo life and history. I saw my share of ruins and dances, trooping through them with the usual museum fatigue that grips us when our interest is still undeveloped. Then the tragedies and inspirations of the '60s broke over us all. For me it meant poverty, depression, divorce, estrangement from beloved children, political journalism, protest and poetry, and year after year piling up between my late adolescence and my not so young adulthood.

Then one summer in my mid-thirties, I found myself for the first time completely present in Chaco Canyon. I was there with my brother-in-law and old friend Jim Rini in a weather of grief: the first of many family deaths in the climate of our minds. The Canyon's directness, its harsh clarity, smoothed the matrix of our confusions. As we approached La Fajada Butte across the desert scrub on foot that afternoon, I felt myself change, literally from one step to the next. In one stride, I felt my whole self become immediately aware of my whole environment. I'd never experienced anything remotely as intense as that connection before. A deep comfort settled into me, a trusting intimacy that has never abandoned me.

It was a matter of relationship—not of me as a thing and Chaco as a thing, but of what was possible between us. In exactly the same way as I am catalyzed by certain friends, by the atmosphere of candor and acceptance that allows me to be more than I imagined or scripted, Chaco permitted me to feel it all and likewise to be felt by it in my entirety. When one feels "in entirety" one doesn't, of course, feel everything; one feels it, as a human can, all at once in shadow form, in suggestion, not as a god who could feel it all in absolute detail. But again, it's the relationship that matters. And I'm more convinced than ever, as the years go on, that it is exactly the same with places as it is with people. Some places make you uneasy, or threaten you and make you want to withdraw. Some are ephemerally pleasant, decoratively pretty, others monumental, gaspingly beautiful or intimidating. Many places simply leave you flat. They have no life for you, nothing to impart. You feel played out when you're in them, used up, or fatally bored. There is nothing more deadening or dampening than being with a person like that either, one who does not catalyze your capacity for imagination and honesty. It's the difference, say, between breakfasting with an old acquaintance who likes you and needs you but who has nothing on his mind and who causes you to have nothing on yours, the difference between that and dining, say, with a windfall friend, someone you never would have expected, someone you met and instantly felt entirely at home with, so that you became completely possible in their presence, and they in yours.

That's how Chaco was for me that first trip with my brother Jim. Its desolate beauty, the galactic slowness of its ruins—ruins of oceans, of fishes, of human beings, ruins of its sea floors and its tallest buildings, of its sky watchers and its sharks, the phantom fullness of its missing days all present in the present now—I sensed them all that day. And I felt that the Canyon understood me—my hiddenness, my desire to be as anonymous as the human lives that once inhabited the Canyon, my attraction to emptiness and to the free safety I feel in dangerous weathers.

The relationship is everything. It's as if the Canyon and I had already experienced the full history of our encounter and were living it now in recollection. This life-changing intimacy with personal landscape and personal friends is like revelation without doctrine, like the experience of mysteries without initiation. So it is not as odd as it might first seem to associate Chaco with friendship and both with the divine. Some of us need hands and warm stones and hot minds to believe. It is like that with deep friendships and intuitive connections. We know each other as if we were each other, which means we do not expect each other to be what we know, but trust each other to be anything we are.

—*V.B. Price*
June 1998, Albuquerque

For Ryan and Talia

CHACO BODY

«I»
TRANSPARENCY

To imagine is to know
with no reference to the truth,
the truth which is without us
only pure.

We believe and we become.

Canyons, kivas, minds,
each contain a space
which is
what has contained it.

Power is in opening
so holy nothing is the way.

The canyon comes to you at dawn,
    as a god comes,
    full of prophecy, funereal,
light as gravity with nothing left to pull,
    as the past
    fills you
    as a void would,
            exploding in
    as sun fills an open eye.

Here one wears the place as one would wear a mask,
is asked to join a dance one does not understand,
and does it,
            knows it,
            is it and is not,
in union
            with both doubt and play,
            and what one makes of doing.

There is no letter of the land,
no gospel code.
The literal means no more that what has formed it
as an instant means no more than what's behind, ahead.
The place is
everything it is,
in time, in mind,
its emptiness
and the front side of its stories.

      Chaco body,
      deep breathing breezes through the weeds,
      rock face changing faces,
            imagination knows
            the present as transparency,
                  deep vanishing,
                  its mask of instants,
            knows
            what is

is constantly not there,
a focusing
emerged into itself,
over and over,
layer by layer,
a black hole, looking glass
which holds it all,
its molecular days,
its oceans, corpses, gods,
its depths and surfaces of light,
the weight
of its transparencies, stratigraphies,
its harmonies of scree clack,
clouds of river foam, their floating by,
shorelines lapping,
sharks cruising through the cliffs,
flood gusts, virga, lightning far as dreams,
and water in the ditches,
the sound of bells, of beaks, of rattle flutter,
the wondering
in living skulls
in spirit face
risen from the light beneath
to stand
in moon air,
hearing still
vibrations
from other worlds, heart drums

in the round soundings of the night
deep underground
where souls diffuse into their flesh
and imagination waits
as possibility in nerves.

Transfigured here,
to imagine is to wear
the mask of endless once,
the canyon
            uttered on your breath
into the space that covers you
as emptiness is covered, instant by instant,
as dreaming
            hardens into sense
so you can vacate where you are,
filled as a mask is filled
with being that is neither
form nor soul
but possibility
worn inside
so you can play at being where you are,
remote, remorseless,
dancing away, unchanging,
circular, in upheaval, straight ahead.

It is dead,
where future dies,
and all around you
you inside
transparent as the lens of now.
And somewhere in the seeing
you disappear,
mind becomes its space,
and your eyes themselves,
are openings in time.

II

ALREADY GONE

Never freed from now,
I cannot hear them,
                I can have
                no memory of their lives.
                Their voices are behind me
    even though I am
        what they have left behind.
                        As if time
        were whole
        and still behind the lives of those
who cannot hear me now,
                I am the heir
        of their imagining,
                and am,
                myself,
                no more
                than what
    cannot be known tomorrow.

In the human now
we know them as ourselves.

It was so
on the walk to La Fajada in the polished heat,

the sun inhaling, holding its breath;
it was so
        when nine
        hundred years
        across the dead sand, scrub, and ants
a clump of grasses whirled and hissed
so violently I felt
the holy panic in myself,
the terror vacancy, adrenal gorging and the dread
to hear
        what must have been
        the passing of a god
        with no one left there
                to believe it.

Believe the fossil fin,
the tide pool ripples on the canyon wall.
Believe divinity filling voids.

Our questions are the same,
formed from stories
    we cannot know,
           stranded in our nows.
    But I say,
    as I read the day,
    that the land has memory,
             that the past must
       come to it,
       that it is

      unconsciousness itself,
that there
we all
    are visitors without guides
        in the un-
        recollected memory
    of the world.

We are the heirs of all imagining.

Because the canyon knows the death I am,
I know myself
as carapace,
      as lightning freed,
      long gone in light,
  as myth again
  which is to truth
      as bodies are to death,
            mortal as rock,
      as dreams passing through rock,
alive
    with dying,
        present
        by being unrecalled,
    a fine silt
    waiting for wind,
          true
          as a god
believed through the grasses.

III

BALANCING ZERO

Breathing in,
                  one pays attention
as water drops
with nuclei of dust
                  add up
to mud clouds piling
                      geographies of breath
                      too great
                      to think across,
inaccessible to feet.

Breathing in,
one pays attention to the day
in rain pools
                upside down,
                the sky
on the surface of the water,
water on the surface of quiet mud,
motion
on the perfectness of light.

Breathing out,
one pays attention to the distances of myth
too great to think across:

                    the canyon floor
a map of matter's inwardness,
a truth so distant
we can only see
                    the edge light of its skin
as we handily traverse it
in our bodies
                    after lunch.

Breathing out,
one pays attention to the slowness all around,
to change we know but cannot find,
to landscape symbols
static as the past,
and dead,
                    though overhead
                    cloudlands go
                    before our eyes,
                            if we look away,
air mud moving
as the land we look from moves.

Breathing,
one pays attention
to the edges
                    of the air,
                    of the eyes that see the air,
                    of the brain that knows the edges

        as they fold and open on
        the edges of our lives;
one pays attention
to the lungs,
to what one thinks of mind,
                of inside horizons
where being has no edges
and the self exchanges with the canyon
all itself
      —the place itself
      as intimate and distant as the brain,
edgeless
to the blood that feeds it
with the air around the mind
and on the surface of our sight,
edgeless to the light of suns
as to the light of nerves
lightning with each word.

«IV»

TRACES

...mind bones...
carcass stones
        of how ideas
               shape themselves through matter...
Dreams of permanence!
"...age under-ate them."
            Rock skin,
human bark
built up by lives
        longing for a cadenced breath
...and order...
        wall face
        shoring time
        by imitation,
                damming change
      with canyon shape,
                   eroding
with raw being
        the ocean of cacophony
        before the rhythm seen by myth:
        Muscle makes it music,
        the patterning of days
        laid down
        by hands,

stone by stone…

Imagination forms the land
into a body for the soul,
armor for the flesh,
a mental nest,
          skull house,
         safe,
            so mind
            can thrive
within a world that it is not, can
come home to it,
            can make it seem
as if the world could shape itself
into a human form,
            a formal friendliness,
            natural as ideas.

Sunlight shines in only ruined rooms.

…roof earth,
cedar shag,
pebbled topsoil overhead…

Moonlight in your eyes inside
is as dawnlight
washing over corpses

caverned by decay.
                    Yet in this
                    anatomy
we see stratigraphy
                    of masonry,
                                   not Venuses in stone,
but layering as beautiful
as the body of the rock
...an icon,
            kachina
            of geography,
of the power
of the land
            which people can transform
            because the land
                                   will
give itself
to people who are not apart.

...ruins now,
spine stone disks exposed
where columns once upheld
the kiva roof weave's
yantra round of trees and weeds
                                   ...room hoards hollow,
roof beams now
holes in stone,

like families are,
and clans and god forms are,
                        squared spaces,
circles,
        in the slowest dancing of the rock.

Bonito, Alto, Chetro Ketl
—not artifacts alone,
                not Parthenons,
but myth shapes of a union
they did not deny.

            ...these bodies of our images.

Imagination bonds
the future,
        past and perfect,
                        where to journey is a trial
of recollection
            as we know
                    that even we
are ruins
of some wholeness
                ...shadows, traces
of relationship,
of fuller harmonies,
potentials,

beautiful
in our mortality
as ruins,
and,
as everything that is
without perfection,
perfect as it is.

«V»
LIKE A ROCK

Imagination is the land.

...muse of water,
   muse of stone,
of holiness that's clothed
in sand and weather,
                    in presence
as it comes to us
                across the mind
to convince us
of realities
more than merely real.

Nightland lifting,
               the canyon
               filling up with light
as minds fill
and fall away,
               fragile
               as the history
of how the grasses move,
blade by blade, second by second.

Intimate land:

      The canyon
is a silence
in the center of a Self
weightless as the silence of the rock,
a silence that is felt
pretending you're not there,
sitting still with stones
    to be weathered by the day,
                 forgetting
who you are,
      lost like friends, dead sins,
      like breath
           that rock time won't contain,
a stone eye opened
as eddies of birds
blow past
    worlds within worlds.

      Behind your sight:
the blackness of the molecules,
topographies of faith,
        distance
dense as stone,
    motionless,
    dangerous with grace,
the silent breathing
of the God of Gods

whose name
        nobody knows.

CHACO ELEGIES

I

THE SAME SWEET FOLLY

There are those to whom we are vermin,
or sources of food, or impediments
along the way
to the "inevitable."
There are days when the sky tries to blow us away,
or drown us or dry us up
and we resist.
We hold in common
this Resistance
to change that discounts us,
holding onto our doors
like ants against other ants
holding on
against trifling horrors,
holding on
to our gardens
our children,
our calm nights,
all of us in Troy,
in Argos, Cuzco,
in Chaco and Hopi,
in Watts, Los Chaves, and East LA,
this family of the homely
clinging to home.

Time is no barrier between us.
We are continuous as the history of air.
In the Resistance
we learn
to want nothing
to be
less important
than us,
to diminish
only
the demon
jerking the hand of the grabber.

II

TIME'S COMMON SENSE

Change
is divine
exercise,
      Her practice,
      Her meditation.
Returning
to an again
which is always
a never,
      I know
      we have looked at the clouds together,
      looked at the stone together,
      have breathed in the night together
      —all of us who have known
      the canyon as ourselves.

At Chaco I know I am not alone.
I know I have heard even Homer
weaving the tides of his stories,
and Sappho singing lullabies alone in the night,
heard the footdrums in Rinconada
like ancient surf through the stone.

This is the place
were the past remains.

Utterly changed,
                the landscape
                is the same.

The future happens so fast,
it's too fast to dread.
                And now
                the future is as good
                as already over again.

That is the teaching of the land,
its way of life,
                a way to be with time,
to become time.
                It is all we can know of Her,
                and a practice to become Her,

a Great North Road, a birth canal,
a way to be born
to life and death
                and home again.

                Where I stand
                they stood;
my body is theirs,
as my body is the boy I was,
as the canyon is the place it was,

new cells,
        new life,
                new being every moment,
always,
always,
never ending.

III

MOTHER OF MYTHS

We read of the Hopi (that's all we can do)
that the dead are clouds,
that the dead rain down their souls on earth,
that life depends on their essence.

I felt a closing when my mother died,
felt the past had pulled itself from my life;
where she was
now was nothing.

    Where did she go?

Is she anywhere more than a sorrow,
more than something gone?

    I am starving for new stories.

I have no heaven for her, no Elysium.
She isn't waiting, in pillows and poppies,
for curtain calls from the gods.

    She is a memory
    I often forget
    has no memory itself.

But at Hopi
the dead never leave.
Rain is soul.
And the souls of Chaco
still feed them.
All history's in the sky,
the crops, their bodies.

    Any meal is a communion.

But my mother and I are as far apart
as I am from faith
in the Fall from grace.

She is like the canyon was on a Tuesday
7,000 years ago, or a Monday just last month,
a detail
in the history of time.

The canyon is
every day it was,
as the species is
every person it has been.

    But she
    is my mother,
    not a day in the shape of stone,
    and I don't know where she is.

She is not in her bones,
not in her ashes I put in the waves.

She is an idea
I have not yet formed
like clouds unborn in the sea.

    I want her home with me. I want
    death, all death, to be
    a right proximity.

In Chaco, at least, I know
the canyon is
where the past remains.

    I know it is not
    only now.

So *can* I say
it is time's common grave,
a mother of myths,
where death conceives, where memory
gives birth to the future?

Can I say she is somewhere there
waiting for doubt to leave?

IV

TRUSTING BLINDNESS

It is always night there.
The holy darkness still exists
without a light to tease us,
teaching us to see
                     with our eyes
                         closed,
trusting blindness with our hearts
                                    as night world visions,
                                    erasing the profane,
                                    replace right now with myth
                                    where time is all at once
the "mountain around
which all moving is done"
                            now and forever
                            without sense,
                            like us,
blind in the truth of hope all-knowing.

It is always night there
and I am not afraid of the dark,
crossing a spine of stone into Walpi,
a guest following guides
                         into the holy past
                         from the holy present,

hoping for new sight,
disappearing into a cloud of snow
                              and reappearing
                              at 2 A.M.
on the other side of the mind
                    to feel
                    imagination dance,
                    blind to reason,
where we,
          brittle with fright,
          abandon fear,
          like children can,
          to trust
in human good
to see us through a universe
we'll never understand,
a universe unknowable except
for masks and faith
                    met at night
                    when all gods walk
                    the wine dark streets
like pilgrims through mountains of the sea.
And right now is
all nows,
          so close
          we feel it
all in our breathing,
in the graying woman

keeping time against her hand
with the braid of the girl she is rocking
in the kiva's grace,
                    right now
                    suspended
                    across ten thousand nights,
a full moon frozen,
lighting holy forms
surging from the dark
to give us candy:
                    our delight
                    their faith
as they dance away
                    though the All
                    Possible Source
                    of now, of all
that was, and all
that never was,
where it is always night,
darker than the middle of the brain,
where no one can see
                    but only trust
that faith
in goodness
            is a kind of sight.

V

JOY WITH NO DIFFERENCE

Practicing the canyon,
I feel my emptiness
forget me
          for a moment longer than it takes
          to change and stay the same.
Practicing to be
the willingness of stone,
the bodylife of ravens
loafing on the clouds,
practicing the canyon,
                    I can see
                    how life and death
                    have no difference to speak of,
                    like one second from the next.
Practicing like this
nothing matters more
than anything,
for all things are
empty as forgetfulness
is full
of its unknowns,
like time is
everything it's been in you, so full
you are

everything
that didn't happen, too.
                                    Practicing and practicing,
you might become the space
                                        and the form around it,
all that's there
and all that's not—
                         the shape of your mind
                         the canyon's shape;
you might fit with it
as bodies fit,
                    as light fits with shadow,
                    as faith, itself, might fit with truth
                    as fate fits with fact.

CHACO MIND

GARDEN MUSIC

On the graves of gardens
in Chaco's inner shore,
    I hear the music of time,
spanning the holy once
from the end to the beginning.

Here I am allowed to know
    the other side
    of mythlessness
behind the empty voices, pageless books,
the blank mask of fact, and all
    our boring horrors,
    purposeless for but gain,
and the snotty
    kisses of power.

On the graves of gardens
    beneath the face of the deep,
I see the other side
    in the mirror of my mind,
    as on the surface of the vanished sea
    or in my own free garden
where the present is
    as it was before

when persons, beasts, plants, the planet, and the gods
    all shared alive
the same living place.

On the graves of gardens
    in Chaco's tidal soul,
I know that now
    is the garden long ago
that always soon will be.

    Here in the presence of the stone,
witness to all the storms,
    memories of the future
allow me to recall
    one canyon morning a thousand years ago
when the first, adored, bright infant green
    surfaced through the bony rubble.

Who saw it first that year,
    bursting up
    through flakes and grit,
    up into the deep sea gray of the dawn
    where I stand now
    in oceans of holy corn
            I remember like ideas
    I've just forgotten?

    Am I the child
who saw it first that spring?

(The front
  and the back
  are part
  of the same.)

On the graves of gardens
    in Chaco's testing grace,
I know the other side
    is now
in truth I cannot say,
    truth I only know
because I trust
    my animal sense of it.

Here in the canyon,
even stone knows
what numbers cannot tell,
even wind knows
what fact denies.
    Here on the graves of gardens
I see myself
at the moment that I die,
dreaming truth about the other side:
                that I'm alive,
                right now,
in gardens
        my dreams
will treat one day
            as holy.

II

THE MUSIC OF TIME

It is all one sea,
one sky,
      to the edge
      of the end.

At Pacific's rim off Malibu,
    sail boats slicing through a sunny fog,
we watched the waters
swallow Chaco up,
and we could see
        no difference
on the surface of the sea.

And as the waves changed places,
the sea between us
was made of ashes
and the air of days,
        days like drops of rain,
like mist, so many days
one after another
        endless
        without beginning.
        (There is
        nothing

more.
There is
nothing
other.)

On Chaco days
    when shirts are sails,
    and wind works dust like water,
I've seen sharks' teeth, like weeds,
cropping up on sandstone flats, have held in my hand
a slab of fish, rock fins and scales flat as shale.
I've seen the nacre of shells, like angel skin
budding through the surface of the rock.

Before "death
and its questionable past,"
I understood so little.
I thought I put my mother's ashes in Pacific Seas,
    released her to the waves
    and she was gone.

But now, the ocean's sound
is just her breathing,
my mind rising and falling
    with the tide of days
    on Chaco's inner shore;
my father's ashes
and my own with hers

rising up in thunderheads
      chasing poets off the cliffs
      with lightning fact
that burns through words
so faith, for once,
      is purified of form.

As ghost clouds
boil across the stone flats
with eons of the moon,
I feel her like a thought
released without a sound,
      and see
no difference
on the surface of the sea.

III

THE CAVE OF GENERATION

We know the past is fiction,
now does not exist,
the future cannot be
till nothing's left of it.
                    We know this
and we don't
know more or less
what we know.
                    We sense
                    the paradox
                    of then,
that flux of tense
                    —the almost now
                    and the lost ago—
these atoms
in the weight of self,
that flood the skull,
                    the theater
                    of our stories,
that cave of time
upon which all
identity depends.
We cannot be without our stories.
Even if we know them to be false

as dreams are real,
they are
where we take place,
                        until the mythless
                        twists them into "truths"
demanding faith
in the false-
            face of acts
            molded clearly over motives
            that falsify the faith,
                                and we retreat,
betrayed
to the cave, the paradox of then,
where first things happen
                        and wait
                        for generation
                        free of force.

We know the mythless world
erases stories
like fanatics reform cultures
by chopping off a million heads.

But caves are not ways out;
they are ways back,
as all beginnings are returns.
                        (Now is
                        a holy
                        place.)

Despite the loss
of all the images of our trust,
some of us each time
take the dark walk
through the cave of the mind
                              and return
                              as the persons
                              we would become,

slowly
broken to the truth,
                    by doing
utterly no more
that what we choose
naturally
to do each day.
                When I return
I arrive at Bonito's
rounded back of perfect bone
the cave of generation,
and feel my attention open
to what I find,
                waiting
for what appears
pure of motive
                as the stone,
                irresistible
as what has happened
just before
            it happens.

IV

WAITING FOR SHOOTING STARS

For Rini, Jim, Jacki, Marc, Chris, John, Francis, and Ian

I have never physically been to the top,
star waiting on La Fajada Butte.
But I would not need to be told
how to be
     if they, long ago,
      should find me there in their minds,
a useless dream shape
from who knows where.
              I know enough.

        (The sacred
        and profane
        are sacred.)

I know that hills and peaks
are the cores
of caves and the deep;
that everything fits;
that the present
is the core of the past—
          so I know
          what is there
          at the top
as a novice knows

what is to be known
in places too holy
for knowing alone.

We go to a hill each New Year's eve,
and watch the sky on our backs among shards,
backed up to rabbit grass knolls,
waiting for shooting stars.
We are children in this,
knowing the truth
without
being it yet.

And I remember there
    the old watcher on La Fajada
waiting and waiting,
working not to wait,
working not to want
                something to happen.

On my back on the hill
    I know I know nothing,
will never know anything else
                    but what I can guess:
that the dream dark sea of space and time
is real
        beyond thought,
that we witness

the edge of a fact vaster than death ever was,
that the whole
                    endless
                    enterprise of the atoms
results in love
as real as the stars ever are.

I need nothing more.
Stars give light;
                    I see it.
Humans love;
                    I feel it.
Proof enough.
                    In the wild, serene,
                    annihilating
                    night,
                    we are real.

                    We belong.

                    We are real.

V

RUNNING TO WIJIJI

When you know who you are
you do who you are,
polishing a mountain

        without a goal.

        (There is
        nothing
        more.
        There is
        nothing
        other.)

At ten,
I did who I was;
I had no choice;

        knowing and doing were not apart;
and where I was
was as much of myself

        as what I did.

        (Now is
        a holy
        place.)

Then years of trying
    and coming apart,
polishing stones
not the mountain
until
    the canyon
      wore me away
so I could see myself

                singular as rocks,
                as shadows, clouds,
                as cliff curves, edges,
                water scars and swirls,
real as skin,
clear as sudden change,
                my body
                opening to the stars
                like Chacra Mesa
                on the skull of the world.

Now at 50,
I am the place again.
                (The front
                and the back
                are part
                of the same.)

At ten, the place
                was a forest street

where I did who I was,
      biking to escape
      tender failures,
sailing through arbors of high ponderosas,
winding like grassy streams
                  through Saturday morning sun.

When you are who you are
you do who you are.
                  (The sacred
                  and profane
                  are sacred.)

At dawn near La Fajada,
breathing in
the rising light,
            I am
ten and 50 all at once.
Running through fossil fields of corn,
running the cool space of canyon shade
as one runs memories through the gorge of time,
I see myself
                  in the shadow at my side,
bike rider, now
                  dawn runner
reaching Wijiji
                  at
                  the
                  moment

the sun
        blooms
wildflower light,
    lightning white
over the canyon rim,
over the edge of my brain.
                    Stunned by God
                    again and again,
why should I doubt
        any longer?

CODA

Now is
a holy
place.

There is
nothing
more.
There is
nothing
other.

The front
and the back
are part
of the same.

The sacred
and profane
are sacred.

ACKNOWLEDGMENTS

I would not have written much about Chaco Canyon had it not been for photographer Kirk Gittings who asked me in 1985 to collaborate with him on a book of poems and photographs that eventually became "Chaco Body." This suite has taken on a number of different forms—a book designed by William Peterson, produced by his Artspace Press, and distributed by the University of New Mexico Press; a fine art portfolio, sold to museums and private collections; and a half hour television production for PBS and KNME-TV in Albuquerque, created by videographer Michael Kamins and introduced by archaeologist Mike Marshall. Because of Kirk's creative generosity, aesthetic genius, and deep attachment to Chaco, I was given the chance over many adventures to be with the canyon as a poet. I had never written about it before in any sustained way, despite a long and intimate association.

After "Chaco Body" was completed, I realized I had another series of poems that loosely related my childhood sense of loss to the Canyon and to my adult experiences with Pueblo people. The result is "Chaco Elegies," which was published in its entirety by John R. Milton in his *South Dakota Review*. But the Chaco work didn't want to end. And so a final suite of poems appeared, entitled "Chaco Mind," which further explores imagination and personal time as they move through the physical life of the canyon. "Chaco Mind" has been accepted for publication by Robert Masterson in his periodical *Manila* produced by the Lords of Language, but has not, at this time, seen print.

Poems from the trilogy have appeared in numerous other publications, including *Blue Mesa Review, Artspace Magazine, New Mexico*

Magazine, and in two anthologies, *New Mexico Poetry Renaissance* and *Saludos: Poemas de Nuevo Mexico.*

There are sixteen poems in *Chaco Trilogy,* the last being a coda which relates the poems numerically to painter Allan Graham's "Cave of Generation," an installation work with literary references to the "Odyssey" and to Porphyry, the neoplatonist Roman author. Much of "Chaco Mind" comes from the context of long discussions during a 27 year friendship with Graham. More recent far ranging and catalytic conversations with the writer, artist and photographer Mary Beath have caused me to re-think the philosophic structure of "Chaco Mind" and have set the groundwork for another offshoot of the Chaco work, a collaborative suite in progress with her of 25 poems and photographs entitled "Mapping the Garden".

As with all my work since 1968, I could not have written a word of it, as it is, without the spiritual strength and immense generosity and love of the artist Rini Price, whose husband and companion I am so grateful to have been for the last 30 years. Most drafts of every poem I've written in that time have benefitted from the candor and acuity of her critical intelligence. My work with her recently on a joint project of paintings and poems entitled "Death Self" has influenced my sense of the Chaco poems as comprising a single body of work.

Finally, I've adventured in Chaco Canyon only with people who matter to me: Rini, my sons Jody Price and Keir Price, my sister Toria Price, my daughter-in-law Amy Price, my nephews Marc Fuqua and Chris Fuqua, child advocate Frances Varela, Kirk Gittings, Gabe and Erika Gittings, old friends Ian McLeod, Francis Roe, Allan Graham and Elizabeth Gordon Walker, J.P. Rini, my brother in law, and Sandra Rae Greenwald, my late wife. I hope to visit there soon with my daughter-in-law Kady Price and my grandchildren Ryan and Talia. Four poet friends have been in my mind as I've written these poems, Lucile Adler, Cecil Robert Lloyd, Charles Tomlinson, and the late Winfield Townly Scott. Each has helped me, directly or by example, to continue working into my 58th year and, I trust, far beyond. If I have any emotion close to regret associated with Chaco Canyon it's that I could never be there in person with my mother Edith Barrett, my father Vincent L. Price, Jr., my childhood mentor Rosalie Buddington, my first editor and trusted friend Roland Dickey, nor the best friends of my youth in New Mexico, now both deceased, the writer/adventurer James Michael Jenkinson and frontier historian Patrick Chester Henderson.

COLOPHON

Set in **Calisto**,
designed by Ron Carpenter (1987)—
a robust and elegant text face with classical
proportions cleanly bright upon the page.
Named after the huntress companion
who Artemis turned into a she-bear,
later gave birth to Pan, and eventually
became the constellation Ursa Major.

•

Book design by J. Bryan

V.B. Price is a poet, journalist and teacher who has lived and worked in New Mexico for 40 years. His poems have appeared in more than 100 periodicals in this nation and abroad. He has written a column in various publications on politics, human rights and the environment since 1971. His recent books include *Seven Deadly Sins* (La Alameda Press); *Anasazi Architecture and American Design*, co-edited with Baker Morrow (University of New Mexico Press); *A City at the End of the World* (University of New Mexico Press). A new book with Baker Morrow, *In the Anasazi Landscape*, is forthcoming from the University of Colorado Press. Price teaches in the UNM General Honors Program and in the School of Architecture and Planning.